The Popper High School Study Book for Cello

VOLUME ONE

ETUDES 1-5

by Cassia Harvey

CHP312

C. Harvey Publications® All Rights Reserved.
www.charveypublications.com - print books & free sheet music blog
www.learnstrings.com - downloadable books & chamber music

for my Uncle Steve
whose thoughtful encouragement at a crucial time
meant everything

The Popper High School Study Book for Cello, Volume One

Table of Contents

Etude No. 1	Page
Part One (measures 1-19)	1
Part Two (meas. 20-27)	6
Part Three (meas. 28-40)	12
Part Four (meas. 41-65)	15
Etude No. 2	Page
Part One (meas. 1-8)	18
Part Two (meas. 9-12)	22
Part Three (meas. 13-20)	26
Part Four (meas. 21-24)	29
Part Five (meas. 25-33)	30
Etude No. 3	Page
Parts One & Two (meas. 1-9, 10-18)	33
Part Three (meas. 19-31)	38
Etude No. 4	Page
Part One (meas. 1-11)	42
Part Two (meas. 12-15)	48
Part Three (meas. 16-19)	50
Part Four (meas. 20-28)	52
Part Five (meas. 29-62)	54
Part Six (meas. 63-76)	56
Etude No. 5	Page
Part One (meas. 1-18)	59
Part Two (meas. 19-34)	64
Part Three (meas. 35-54)	67
Part Four (meas. 55-73)	70
Part Five (meas. 74-103)	75
Complete Etudes	Page
Etude No. 1	78
Etude No. 2	80
Etude No. 3	82
Etude No. 4	84
Etude No. 5	86

This book divides the first five of Popper's Etudes, Op. 73, for the cello into short sections and provides exercises for the mastering of each section.

The exercises are written to benefit both the professional and the student.

Notes are often repeated to develop agility. **Shifts** may be repeated to help with acquiring muscle memory. **Double stops** are included for establishing relative pitch and building left-hand strength.

Popper's etudes have a strong focus on playing across strings and learning the fingerboard as a grid. These exercises highlight this original intent of the etudes by teaching the notes across strings in the higher positions and helping cellists work on their knowledge of the entire fingerboard.

Tips

After playing the initial short etude excerpt, play the exercises that follow it. Pay particular attention to the concept being studied, which is described in the title. After playing all the exercises that follow an etude excerpt, return to the excerpt and play it. Repeat exercises for any section that still gives you difficulty. After an etude has been studied in sections, turn to the back of the book and play the entire etude.

These exercises give the advanced cellist Popper's etudes with a new, clearly mapped path to technical mastery. By combining the etudes with the exercises, the positions on the fingerboard, that Popper cared so much about, can be perfected. This book is useful for student cellists preparing to perform the etudes in auditions and for professional cellists working to achieve the very highest levels of their art.

The Popper High School Study Book for Cello, Part One

Note: The etudes are broken up into sections in this study book. The complete etudes are at the back of the book.

Etudes by David Popper
Exercises by Cassia Harvey

No. 1
Part One: Measures 1-19

©2016 C. Harvey Publications All Rights Reserved.

String Crossing Work
First play this exercise Détaché and then Spiccato

1. Détaché (legato)

2. Spiccato

Shifting Practice
Measures 1-19

First play as written, then play the following exercises with a dotted quarter, eighth note rhythm:

continued

Double Stops for Intonation: Measures 5, 12-19

The Popper High School Study Book for Cello, Part One

Intensive Intonation Workout in Double Stops
Measures 1-19

©2016 C. Harvey Publications All Rights Reserved.

No. 1
Part Two: Measures 20-27

Learning the Notes
Measures 20-21

The Popper High School Study Book for Cello, Part One

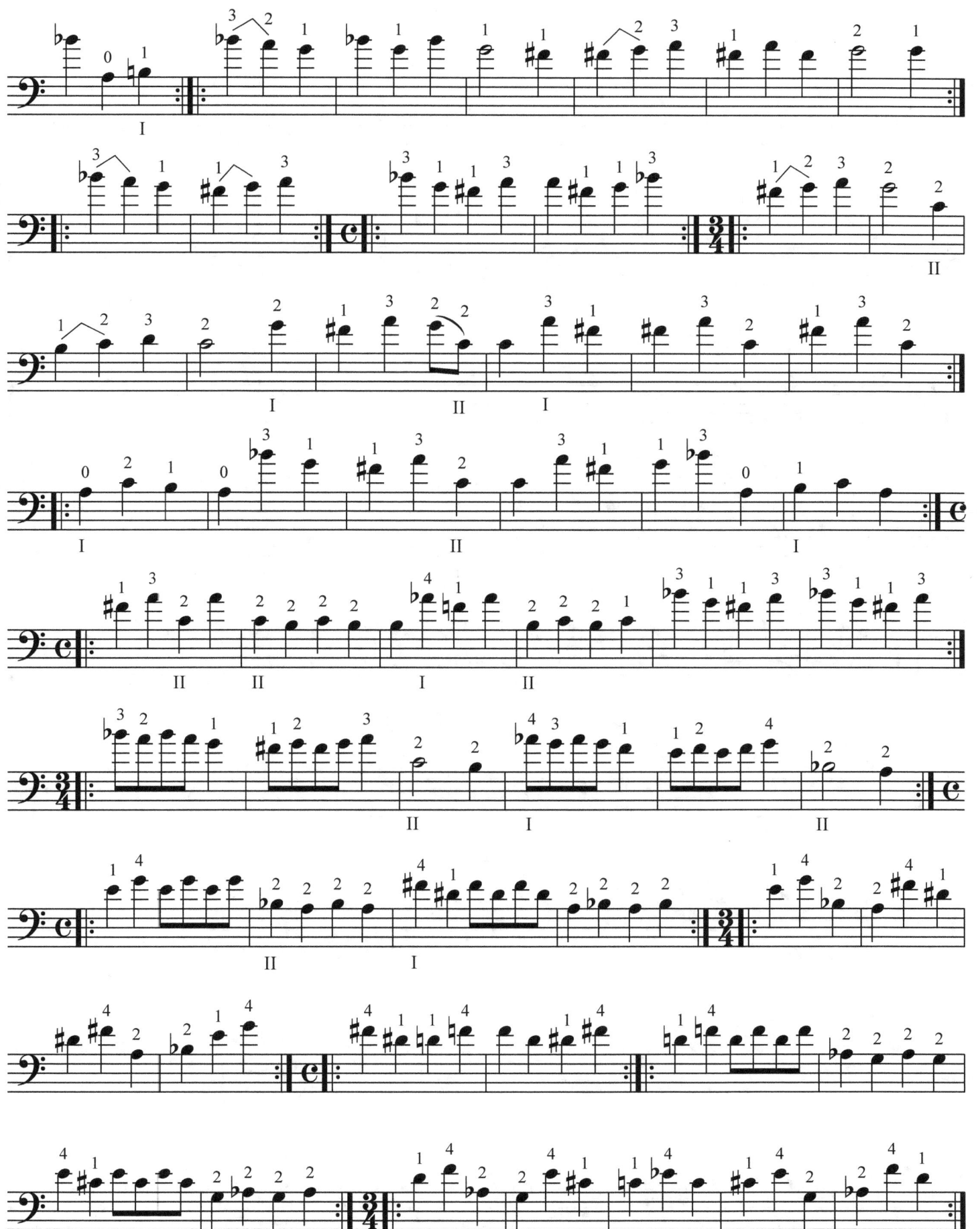

©2016 C. Harvey Publications All Rights Reserved.

Learning the Notes
Measures 22-23

The Popper High School Study Book for Cello, Part One

©2016 C. Harvey Publications All Rights Reserved.

Learning the Notes
Measures 24-25

Learning the Notes
Measures 26-27

The Popper High School Study Book for Cello, Part One

Double Stops for Intonation: Measures 20-27

Fluency: Measures 20-27

©2016 C. Harvey Publications All Rights Reserved.

No. 1:
Part Three: Measures 28-40

Learning the Notes
Measures 28-30

Double Stops
Measures 28-31

Learning the Notes
Measures 32-36

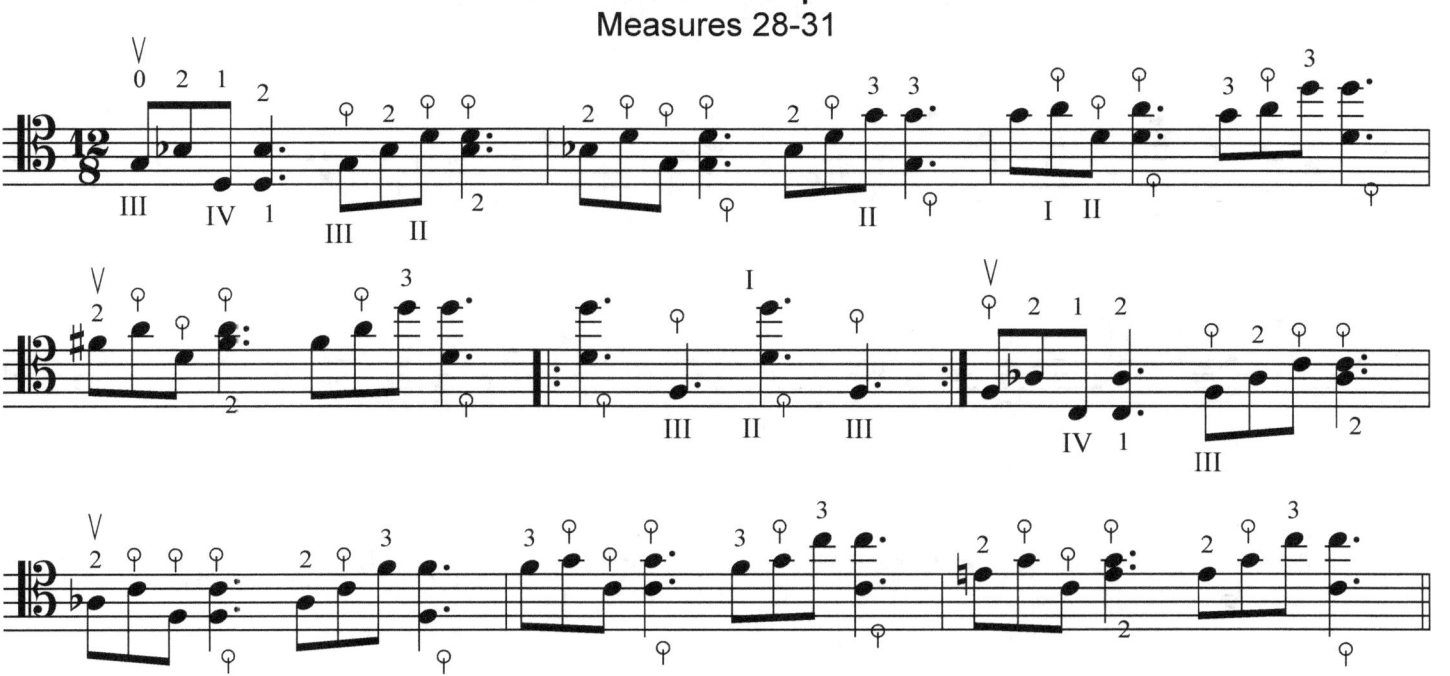

Double Stop Study for Intonation
Measures 27-36

Shifting Study
Measures 37-40

No. 1:
Part Four: Measures 41-65 (end)

Note: Measures 41-57 are identical to measures 1-17.
See pages 2-5 of this book to work on them.

Playing Across Strings:
Measures 59-65

Variation 1 to Work on Spiccato
Measures 41-52
This variation could be played on the entire etude.

©2016 C. Harvey Publications All Rights Reserved.

The Popper High School Study Book for Cello, Part One
17

Variation 2 to Work on Spiccato
Measures 50-54

Variation 3 to Work on Spiccato
Measures 59-62

©2016 C. Harvey Publications All Rights Reserved.

No. 2

Part One: Measures 1-8

Staccato for String Crossing
Measures 1-8

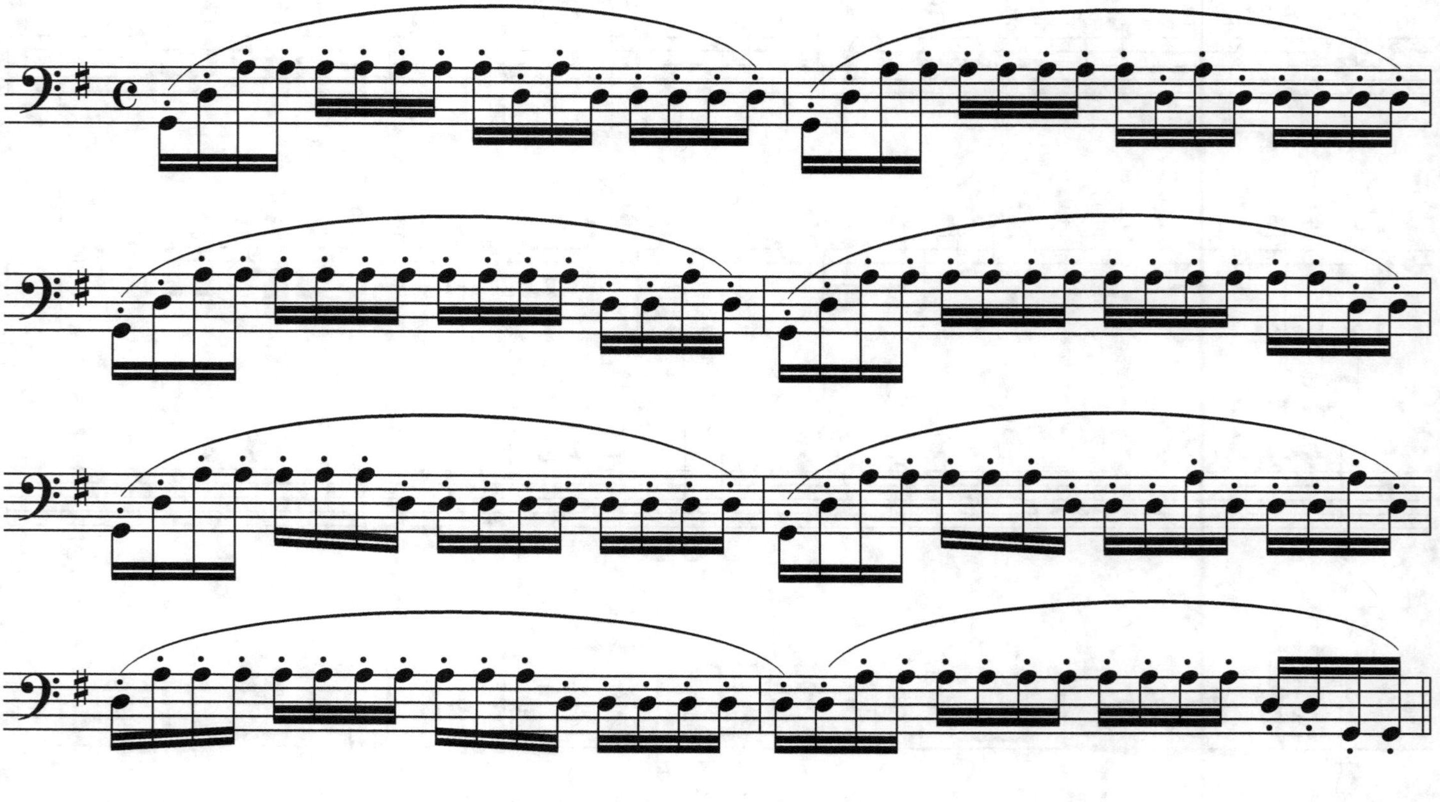

The Popper High School Study Book for Cello, Part One   19

Open Strings
Measures 1-8

Shifting
Measures 3-8

continued

©2016 C. Harvey Publications All Rights Reserved.

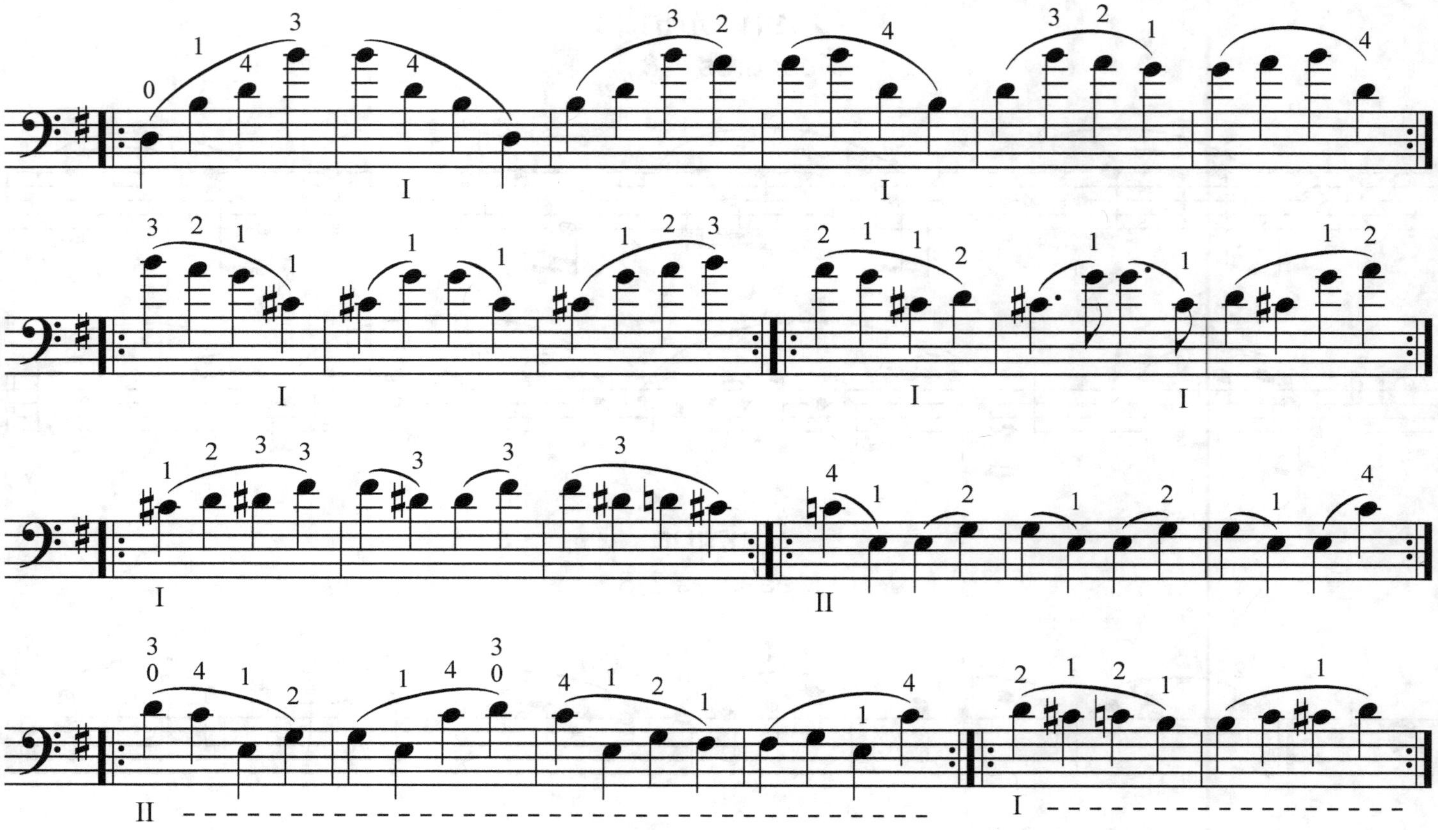

Double Stops for Intonation and String Crossing
Measures 1-8

1. play with separate bows.
2. play with one measure in a bow.
3. play as written.

Finger and Bow Study
Measures 1-8

No. 2
Part Two: Measures 9-12

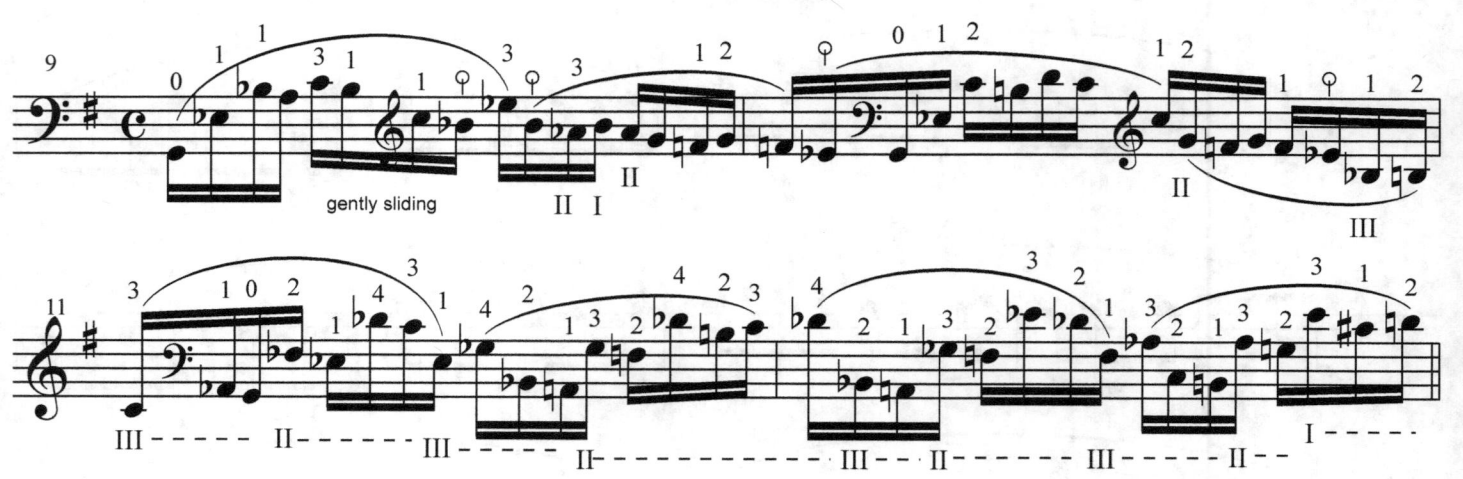

Shifting Practice and Learning the Notes
Measure 9

Shifting Practice and Learning the Notes
Measure 10

Shifting Practice and Learning the Notes
Measure 11

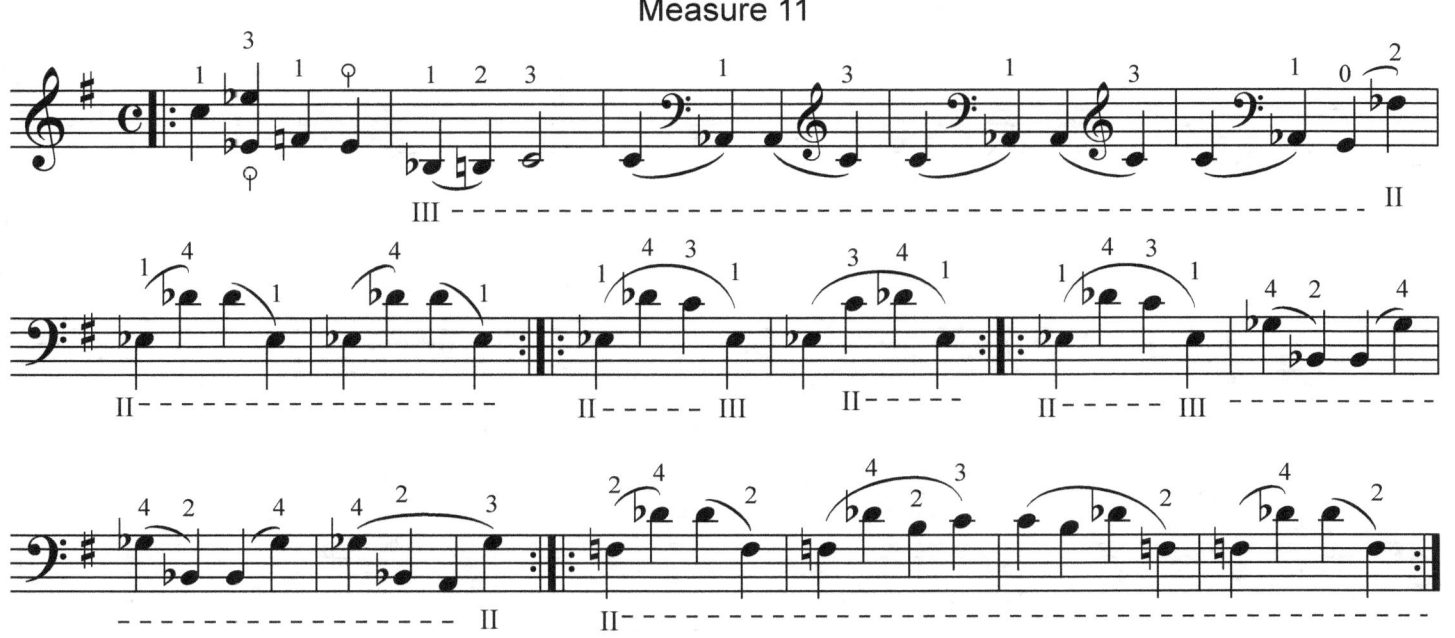

Shifting Practice and Learning the Notes
Measure 12

Starting to Put it All Together

Measures 9-12: First play with separate bows, then play with the written slurs.

The Popper High School Study Book for Cello, Part One

Working on Connections
Measures 9-12

Staccato for Even Notes
Measures 9-12

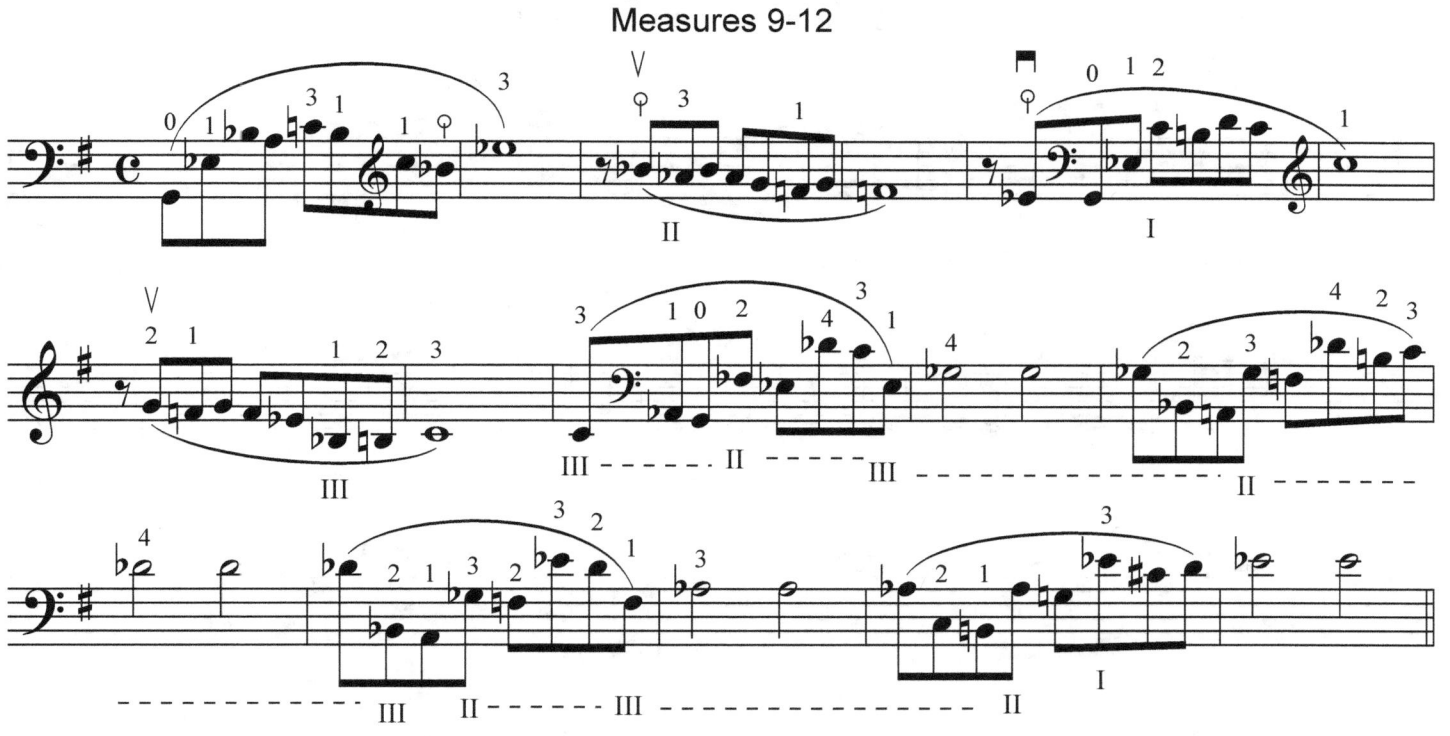

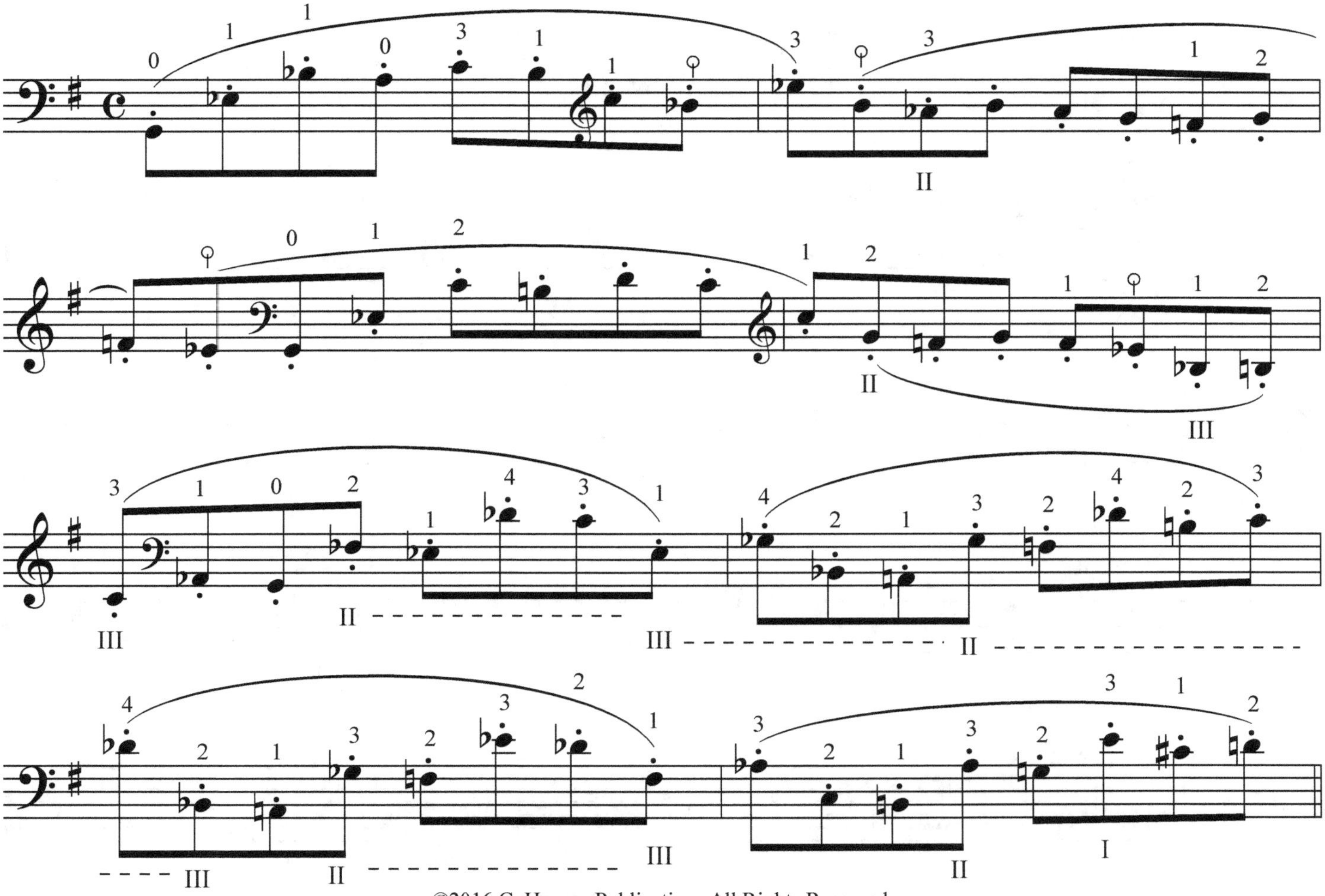

©2016 C. Harvey Publications All Rights Reserved.

No. 2
Part Three: Measures 13-20

Practicing the Shifts
Measure 13

©2016 C. Harvey Publications All Rights Reserved.

Learning Patterns
Measures 13-14

Double Stop Patterns
Measures 15-16

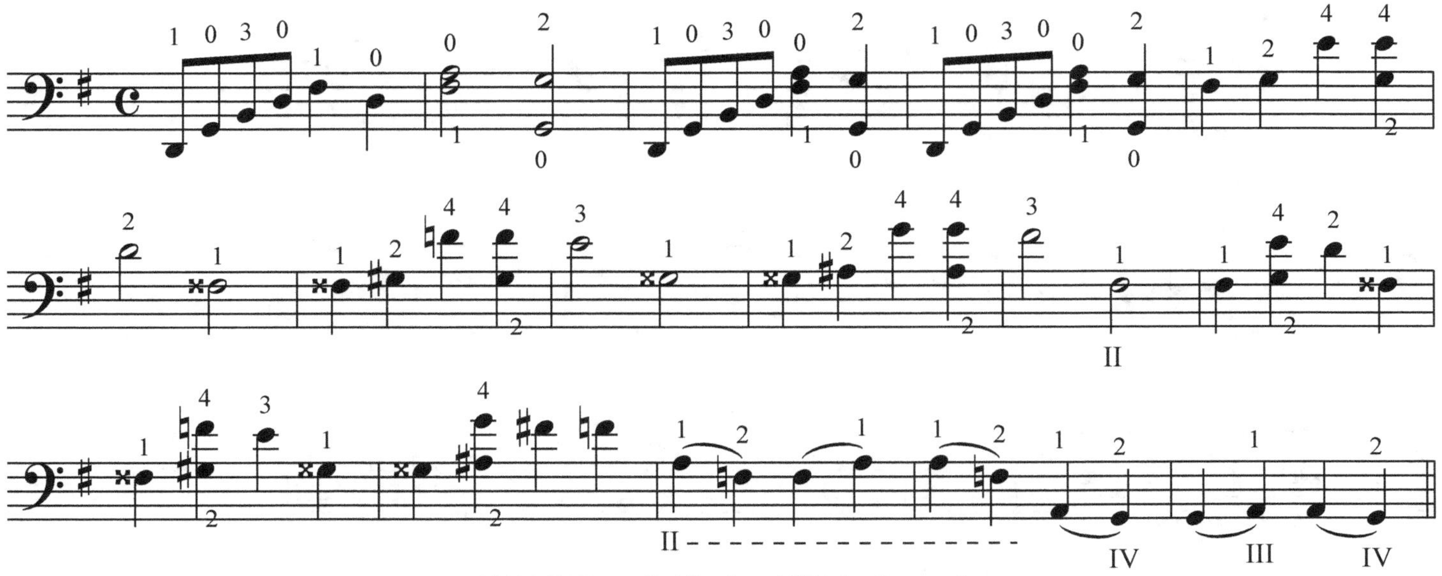

No. 2
Part Four: Measures 21-24

Finger Patterns
Measures 23-24

No. 2
Part Five: Measures 25-33 (end)

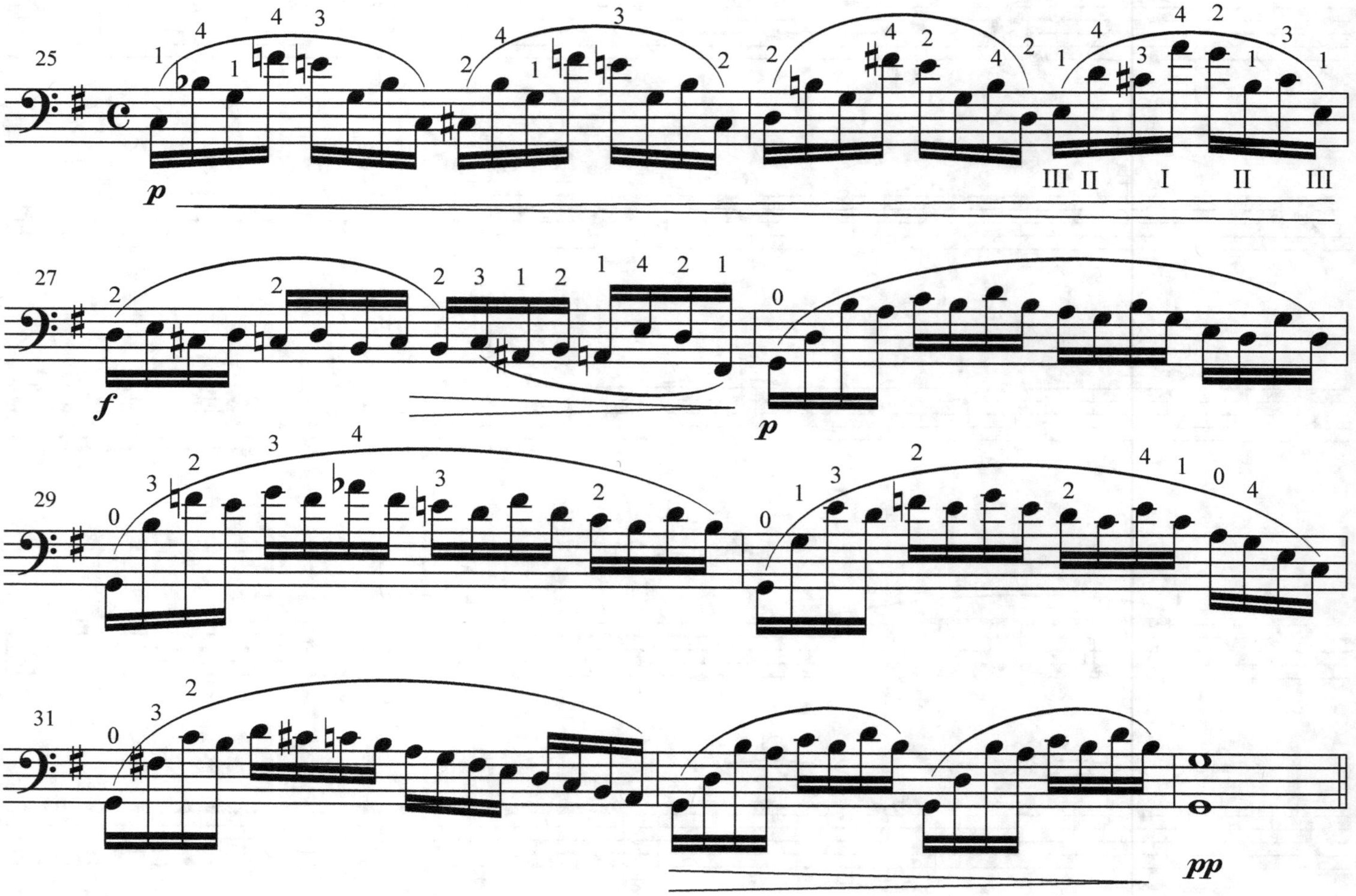

Learning the Notes
Measures 25-27

Double Stops for Intonation
Measures 25-27

Learning the Notes
Measures 29-30

String Crossing Practice
Measures 28-32

No. 3
Parts One & Two: Measures 1-9 (Measures 10-18 are identical)

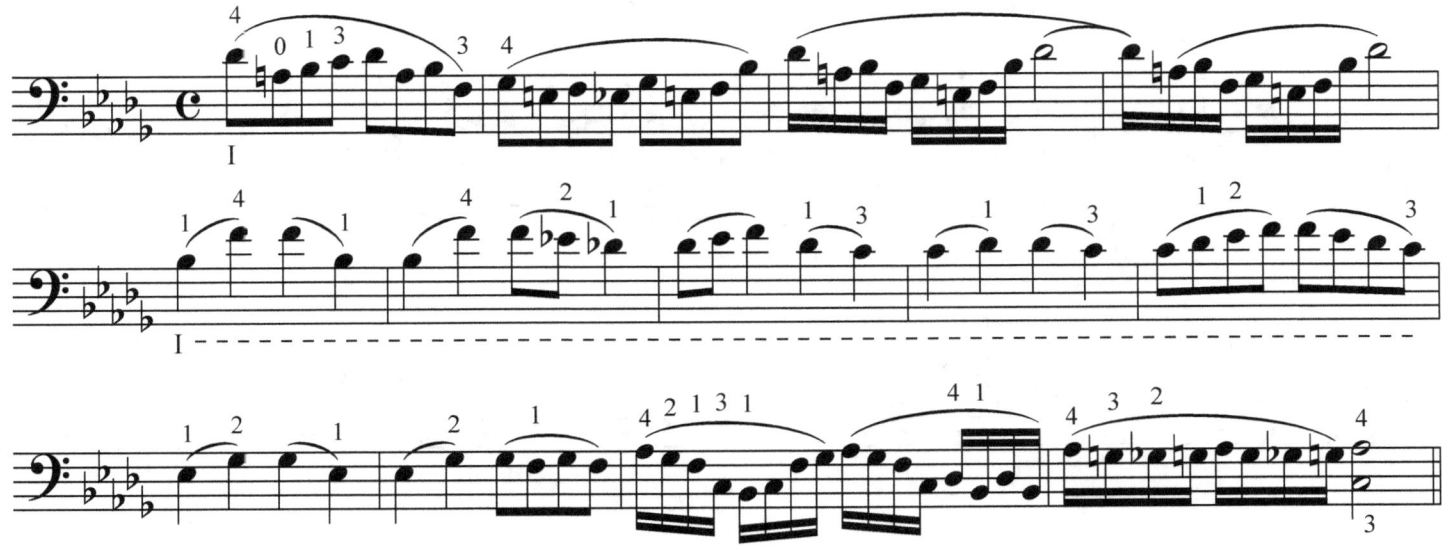

(This fingering is in measure 18 and is the transition into measure 19).

Learning the Notes
Measures 1-2

Finger Patterns and Shifting
Measures 3-9, 18

Double Stops for Intonation
Measures 1-8

Double Stops and Finger Exercises
Part Two: Measures 5-8

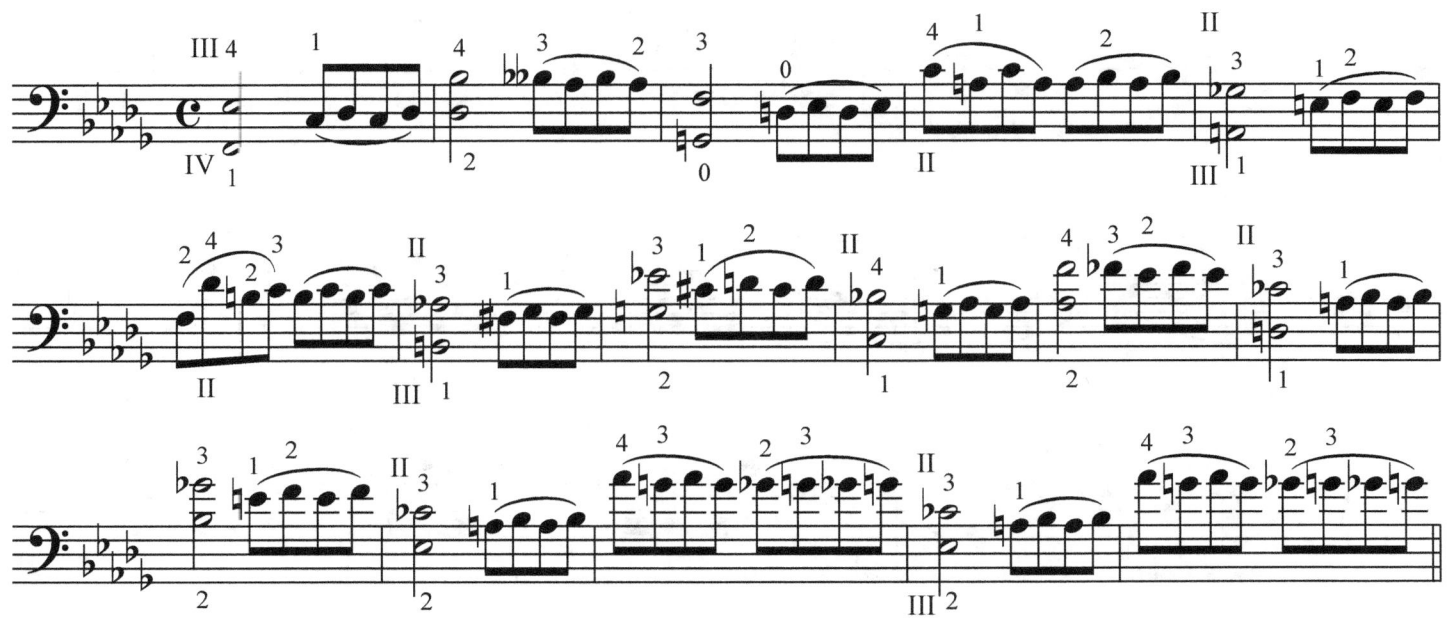

Working on Fluency
Measures 1-18

No. 3
Part Three: Measures 19-31

Shifting
Measures 19-22

The Popper High School Study Book for Cello, Part One

Shifting Studies
Measures 24-30

Double Stop Studies
Measures 19-21, 25, 27, 28

©2016 C. Harvey Publications All Rights Reserved.

Working on Fluency
Measures 19-28

Rhythm Study for Even Fingers and Tone
Measures 19-31

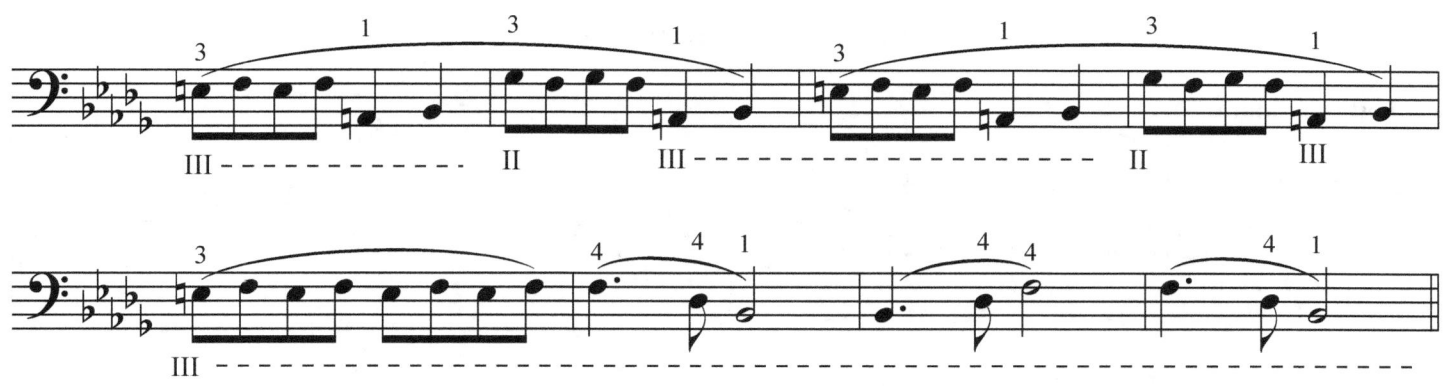

No. 4
Part One: Measures 1-11

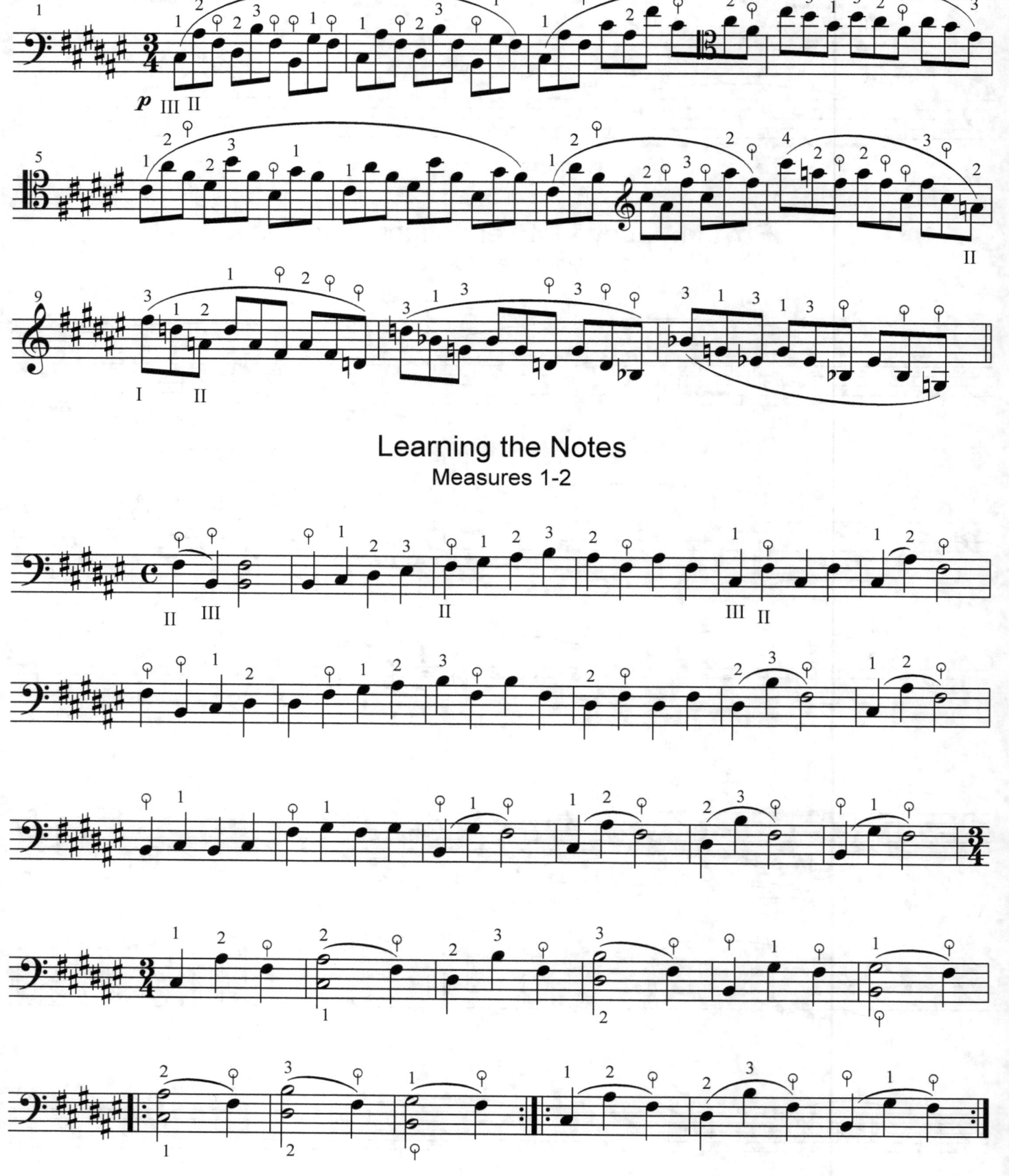

Learning the Notes
Measures 1-2

Learning the Notes
Measures 3-4

Double Stops and Shifting
Measures 3-4

Learning the Notes
Measures 5-6

Learning the Notes
Measure 7

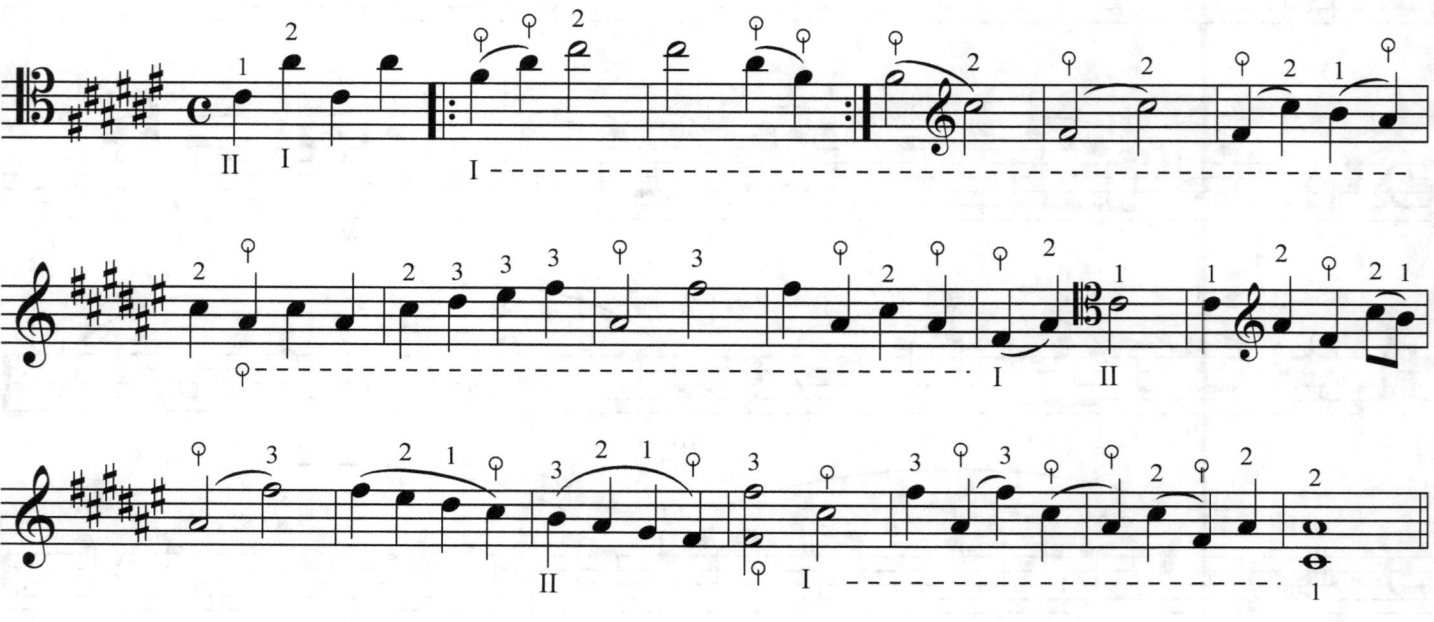

Learning the Notes
Measures 7-8

Shifting
Measures 7-8

Connections
Measures 7-8

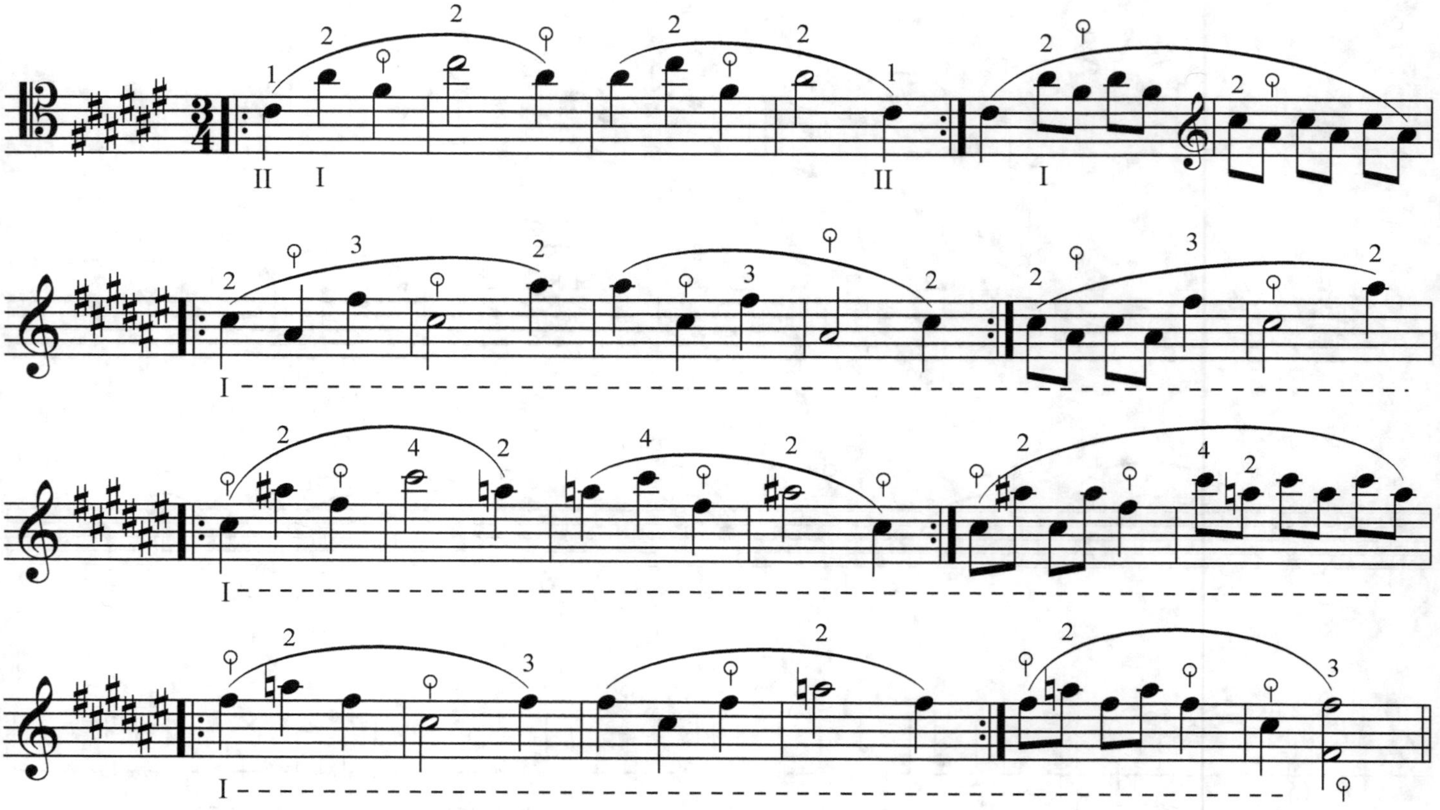

Putting it all Together
Measures 7-8

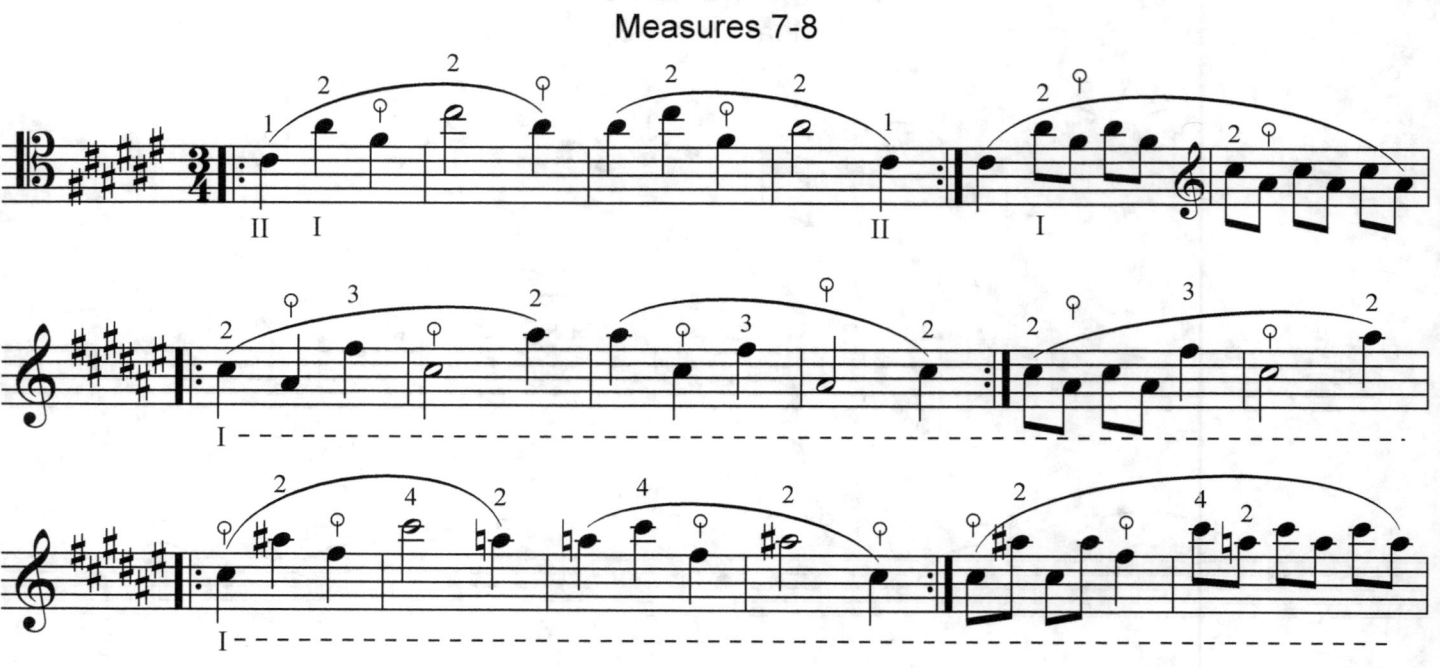

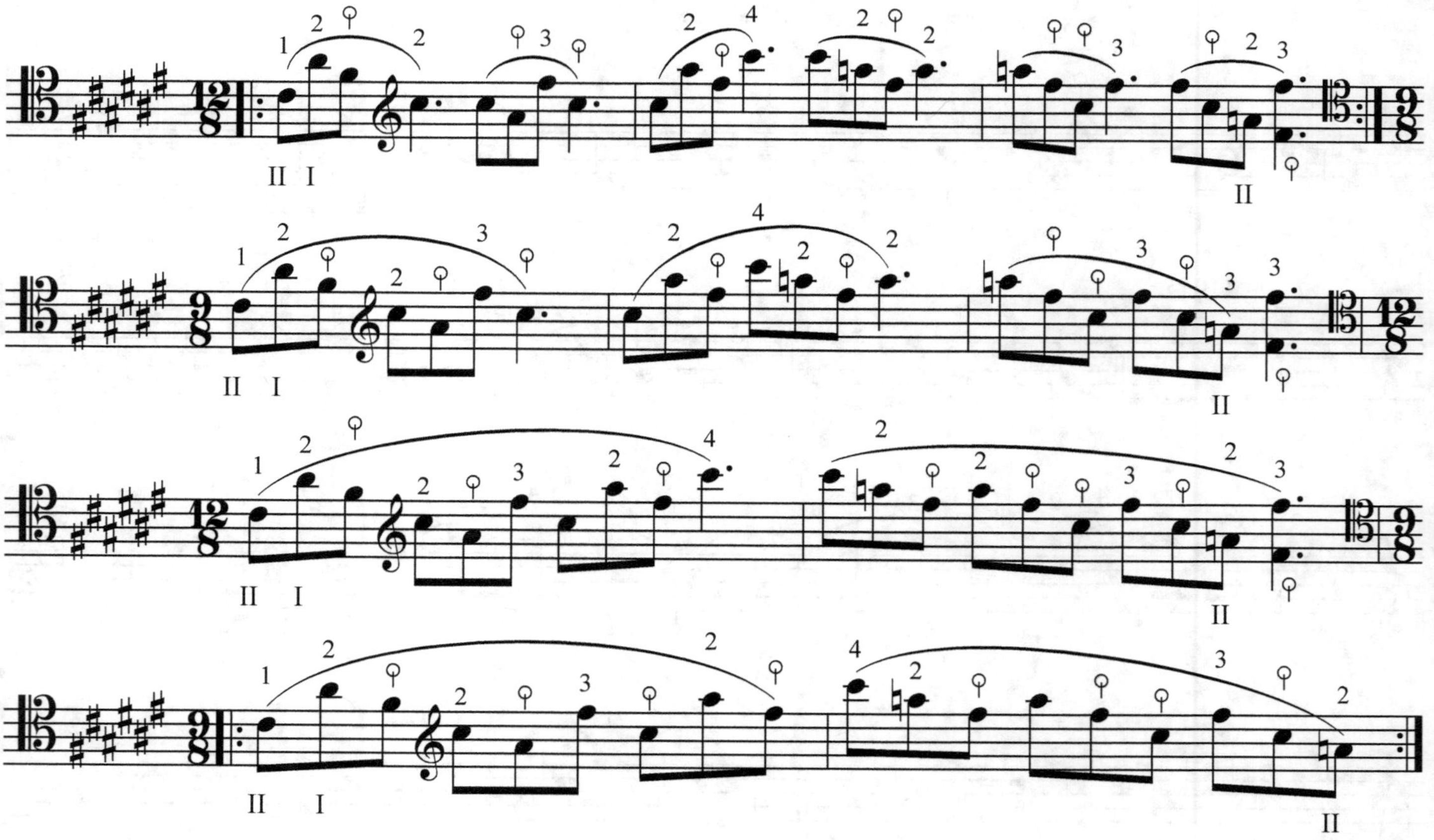

Learning the Notes
Measures 9-11

Fluency
Measures 9-11

48

No. 4
Part Two: Measures 12-15

Learning the Notes
Measures 12-13

©2016 C. Harvey Publications All Rights Reserved.

Learning the Notes
Measures 14-15

Fluency
Measures 12-15

No. 4
Part Three: Measures 16-19

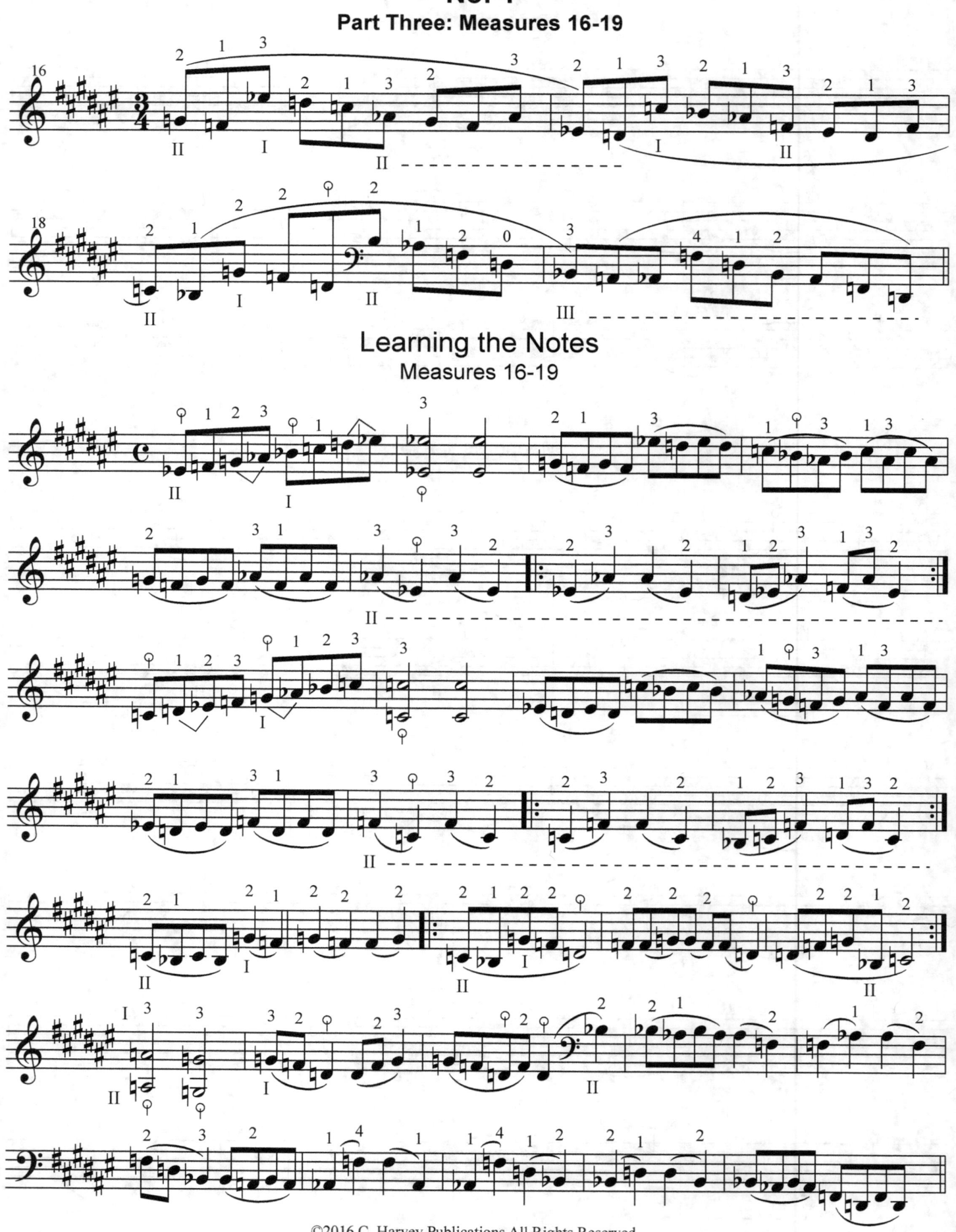

Learning the Notes
Measures 16-19

Fluency
Measures 16-19

No. 4
Part Four: Measures 20-28

Shifting and Double Stops
Measures 20-22

Learning the Notes
Measures 22-25

No. 4
Exercises for Part Five: Measures 29-62 are identical to measures 1-28

©2016 C. Harvey Publications All Rights Reserved.

String Crossing
Measures 1-12, 29-40

No. 4
Part Six: Measures 63-76 (end)

Learning the Notes
Measures 63-66

Learning the Notes
Measures 65-68, 73, 74

Fluency
Measures 63-end

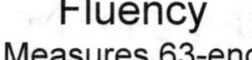

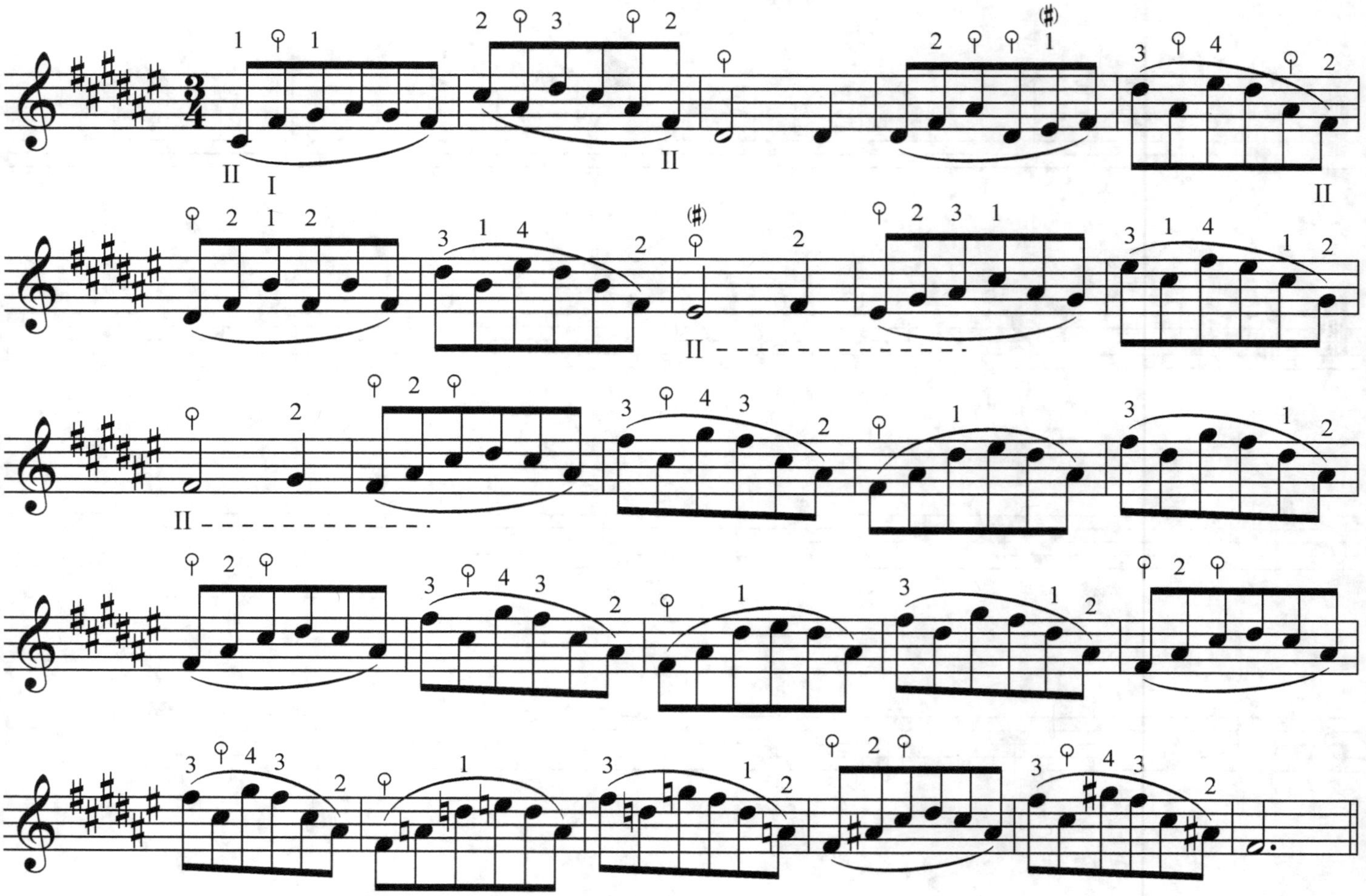

Study
Measures 63-end

The Popper High School Study Book for Cello, Part One 59

No. 5
Part One: Measures 1-18

Learning the Notes
Measures 1-5

©2016 C. Harvey Publications All Rights Reserved.

Learning the Notes
Measures 7-8

Octaves
Measures 9-14

Learning the Notes
Measures 9-15

No. 5
Part Two: Measures 19-34

Shifting
Measures 19-34

The Popper High School Study Book for Cello, Part One
65

Shifting
Measures 19-26

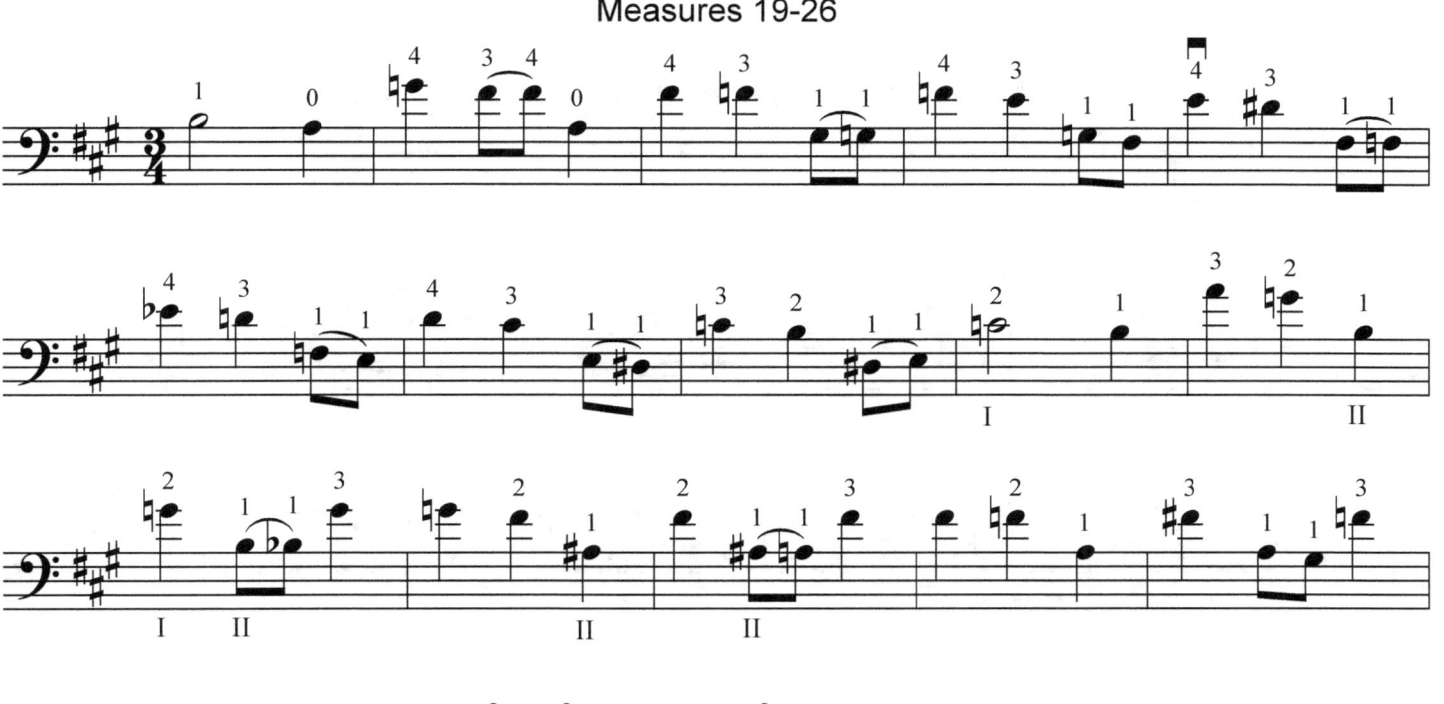

Sixths
Measures 19-34

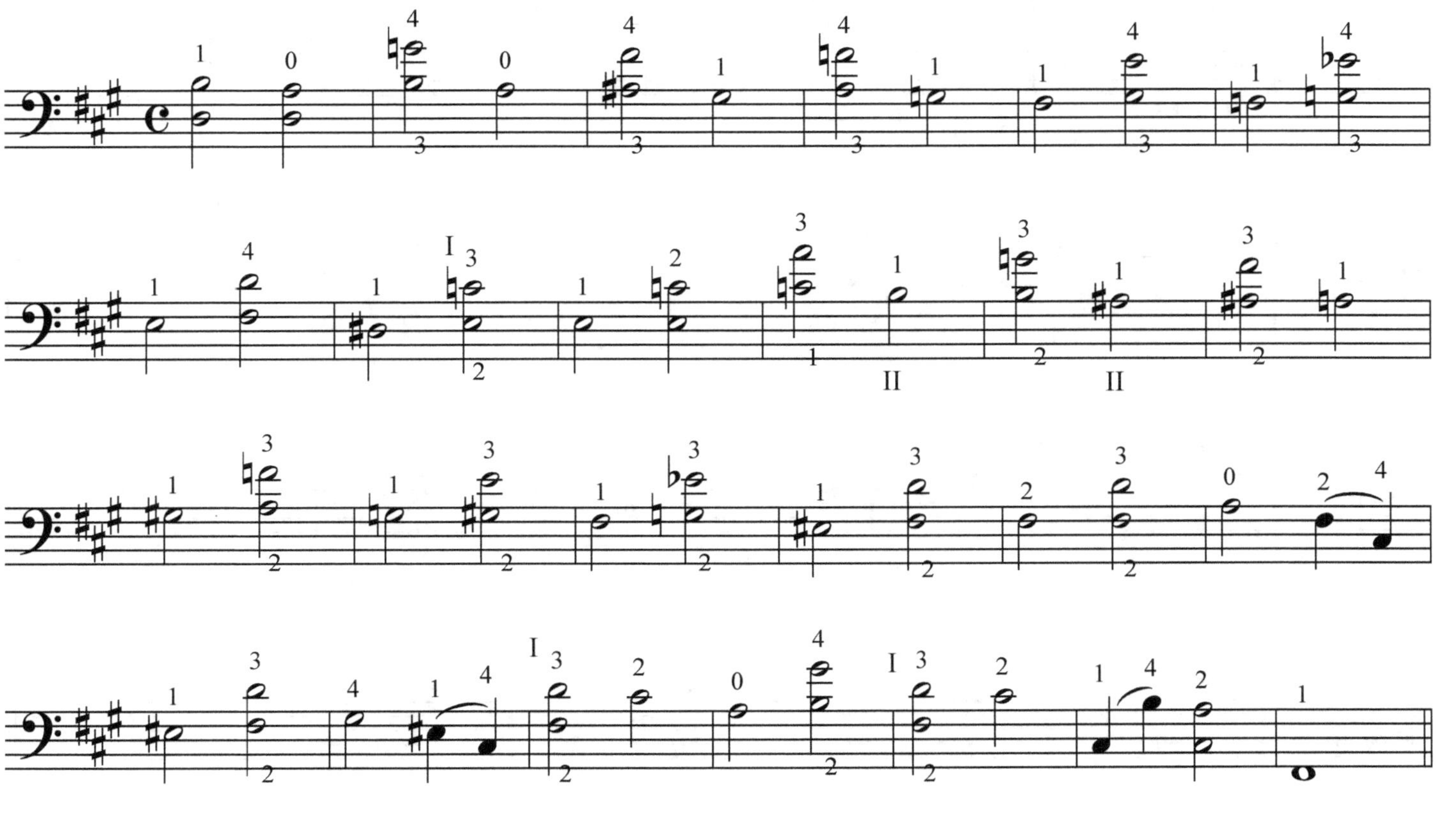

©2016 C. Harvey Publications All Rights Reserved.

Fluency
Measures 19-34

Intonation
Measures 19-34

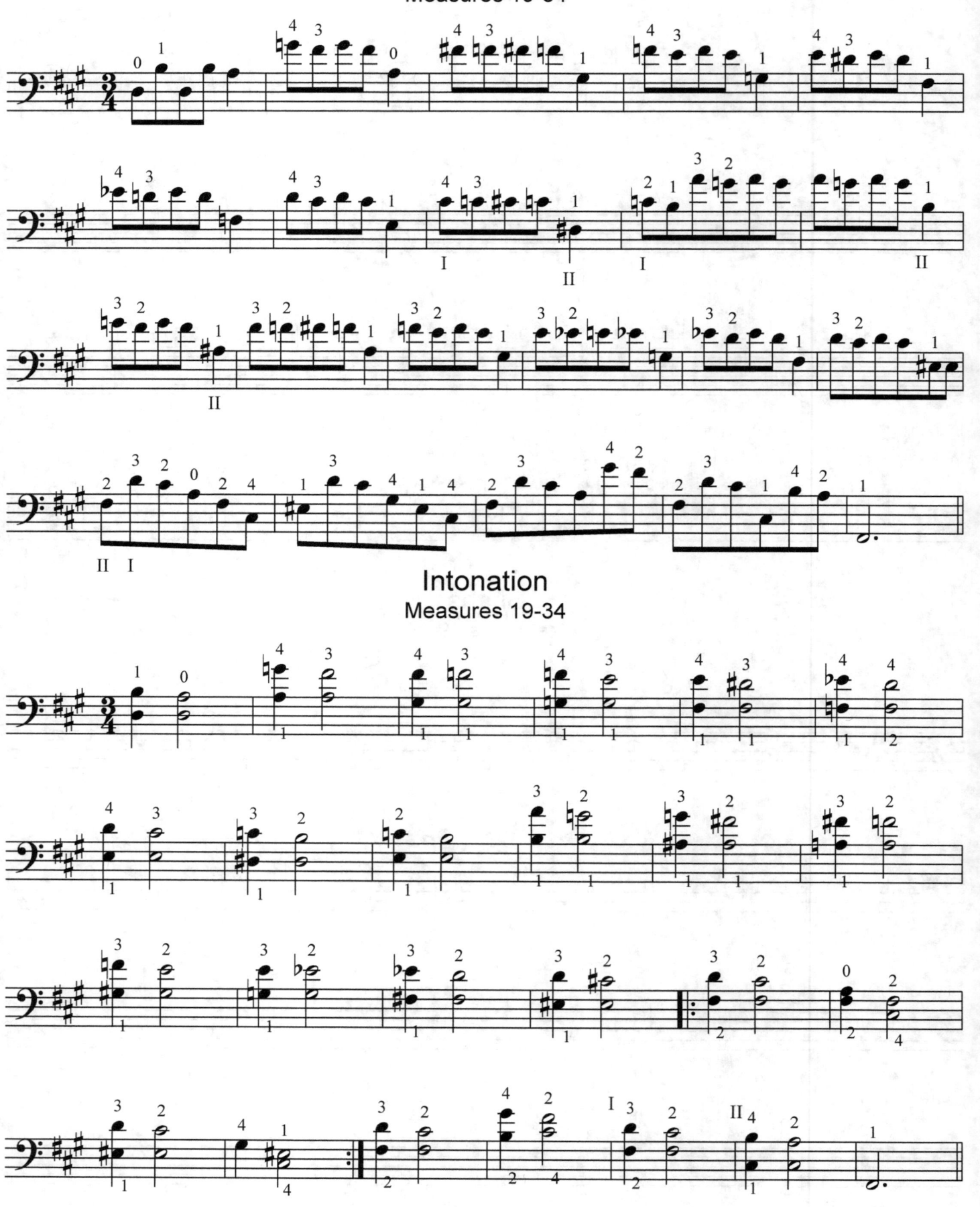

No. 5
Part Three: Measures 35-54

String Crossing
Measures 37-48

Agility
Measures 34-54

Bowing Intensive
Measures 34-40

Shifting
Measures 45-53

Double Stops
Measures 34-44

No. 5
Part Four: Measures 55-73

Learning the Notes
Measures 56-60

Shifting
Measures 60-61

Shifting
Measures 62-63

Fluency and Octaves
Measures 55-73

Learning the Notes
Measures 66-73

©2016 C. Harvey Publications All Rights Reserved.

The Popper High School Study Book for Cello, Part One 73

Solidifying the Positions
Measures 66-73

Focus on Shifting
Measures 66-73

©2016 C. Harvey Publications All Rights Reserved.

Sixths
Measures 66-73

Double Stops
Measures 66-73

Putting It All Together
Measures 66-73

No. 5
Part Five: Measures 74-103 (end)

String Crossing
Measures 74-79

Rhythm Study
Measures 80-103

Double Stops
Measures 74-81

Double Stops
Measures 82-87

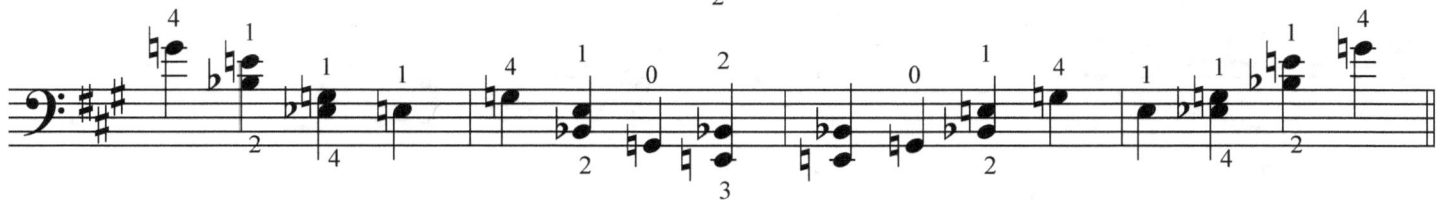

Arpeggio Run
Measures 101-103

©2016 C. Harvey Publications All Rights Reserved.

Etude No. 1

Allegro Molto Moderato — With very loose wrist, at the nut, lightly staccato

Etude No. 2

Andante

The Popper High School Study Book for Cello, Part One
81

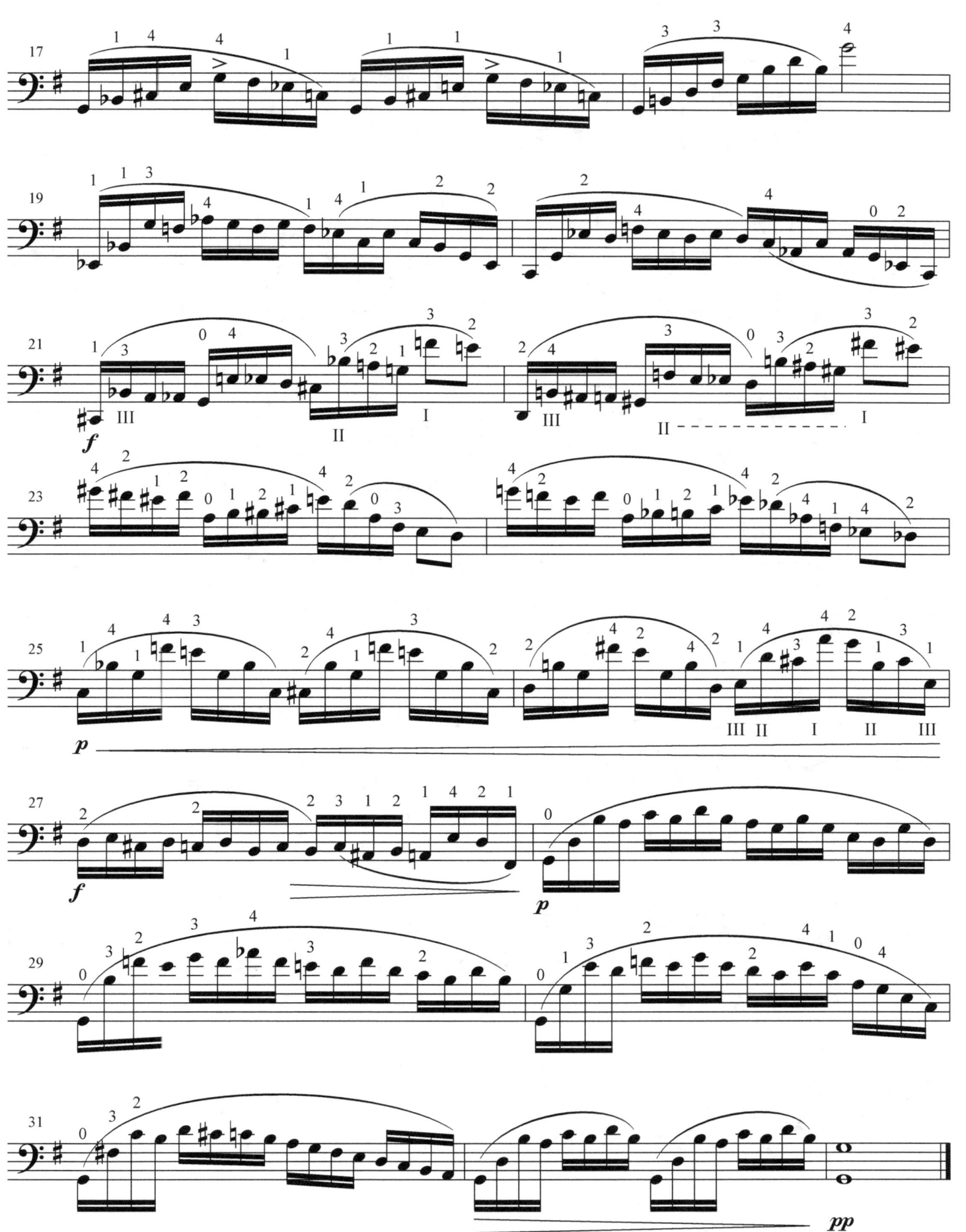

Etude No. 3

Andante

The Popper High School Study Book for Cello, Part One 83

Etude No. 4

The Popper High School Study Book for Cello, Part One

Also available from www.charveypublications.com: CHP435
Open String Bow Workouts for Cello, Book Three

This book of new and exciting bowing workouts for the cello gives you a set of all-new exercises to train your bow on open strings before you begin the rest of your practice.

Since there are no left hand notes, you can focus entirely on improving the dexterity and control of the right (bow) hand.

The main focus of Book Three is bow control. The exercises in this book help you develop bow control using long, sustained bow work, string crossing, staccato, and spiccato, as well as special exercises for bow starts and bow landings.

www.ingramcontent.com/pod-product-compliance
Lightning Source LLC
Chambersburg PA
CBHW051420070526
44584CB00023B/3516